MY TOURIST GUIDE TO
THE SOLAR SYSTEM
AND BEYOND

LEWIS DARTNELL

LONDON, NEW YORK, MELBOURNE,
MUNICH, AND DELHI

Senior editor Ben Morgan
Senior art editor Smiljka Surla
Editor Sam Priddy
US Editor Margaret Parrish
Designer Riccie Janus
Assistant designer Anna Reinbold
Illustrators Katie Knutton, Maltings Partnership
Production editor Joanna Byrne
Production controller Erika Pepe
Managing editor Julie Ferris
Managing art editor Owen Peyton Jones
Publisher Sarah Larter
Associate publishing director Liz Wheeler
Art director Phil Ormerod
Publishing director Jonathan Metcalf

The author, Dr. Lewis Dartnell, is an astrobiologist
and science writer at University College
London's Centre for Planetary Sciences, UK.

First published in the United States in 2012 by
DK Publishing
375 Hudson Street
New York, New York 10014

A catalog record for this book is available from
the Library of Congress.

ISBN 978-0-7566-8994-0

Printed and bound in China by Hung Hing
Discover more at
www.dk.com

CONTENTS

GET READY TO BLAST OFF

You're about to leave for the vacation of a lifetime: a trip into outer space to see the wonders of the solar system. You'll be spending most of your time on an interplanetary cruise ship. Space journeys can last months, but don't worry—your ship is packed with features to keep you from getting bored and to help you stay fit and healthy in zero gravity.

Recreation sphere
In zero gravity you will be weightless. Dance and play crazy games while floating in the recreation rooms.

Toilets
In space, toilets work like vacuum cleaners, and the waste water is recycled so you can drink it again.

Swimming pool
This room contains a large blob of water for space tourists to swim in.

Bedrooms
Rooms are small and consist of little more than a bed strapped to the wall.

Bridge
The ship's main controls are located at the front of the ship.

Observation dome
Sit back and enjoy amazing views of the solar system.

Crew quarters
Living areas are located toward the front of the ship—away from the nuclear reactor.

Restaurant
Tables and chairs in the restaurant are bolted to the floor to stop you from flying away when you're eating.

Communications dish
This dish sends signals back to Earth so you can keep in touch with friends and family.

SUN

MERCURY

VENUS

EARTH

MARS

ASTEROID BELT

JUPITER

Rotating section
This section spins around to generate artificial gravity.

Greenhouse
Plants are grown under artificial light to supply food for long journeys.

Fuel tanks
Spaceship fuel is kept in several large cylinders outside the craft.

Main engines
Large rocket thrusters propel the spaceship through the solar system.

Nuclear reactor
This provides electricity, since your ship will fly too far from the Sun to generate solar power.

Storm shelter
This room has thick walls and no windows to shield you from sunstorms and cosmic rays.

Gear room
A storage room for spacesuits and other items of gear you'll need when you venture out of the spaceship.

Landing craft
The lander is for visiting the surface of planets and moons while the main ship stays in orbit.

Gym
Spend a few hours every day exercising to prevent your muscles wasting away in zero gravity.

 SATURN

 URANUS

 NEPTUNE

 PLUTO

 COMET

 NEBULA

 RED GIANT

BLACK HOLE

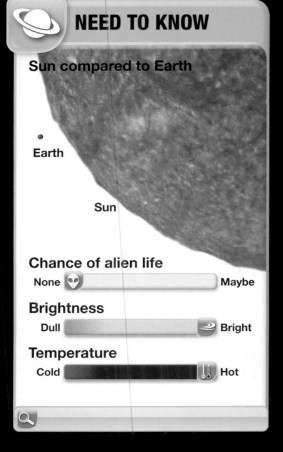
Dark spots
Sunspots are cooler, darker regions that can be many times larger than planet Earth. They are not that cool though— temperatures can still reach 7,200°F (4,000°C).

Atmosphere
The Sun's atmosphere, or corona, stretches for millions of miles into space.

SUN

OUR NEAREST STAR

▶ Journey time from Earth: **1 Earth year**

The Sun is our local star. All the planets of the solar system orbit around it. This gigantic ball of superheated gas (plasma) is a searing 9,900°F (5,500°C) at its dazzlingly bright surface. So, for all but the most intrepid adventurers, the Sun is best appreciated from a distance.

THIS STAR PASS ENTITLES THE HOLDER TO A SIZZLING SIX-WEEK STAY EXPLORING THE SUN. SOLAR IMMIGRATION.

SUN
MAY 28, 2061

6

YOU ARE HERE

SUN

 MERCURY

 VENUS

 EARTH

 MARS

 ASTEROID BELT

 JUPITER

Fiery display
The huge eruptions of plasma in a sunstorm can cause electrical interference back on Earth.

Every day is a sunny day at the solar system's star attraction

Your spaceship will need a **protective shield,** since the Sun gives off harmful **ultraviolet** and **X-ray** radiation.

TOURIST TIP

Solar cruise

"Hot stuff!
Our ship needed a special sunshade to protect our eyes from the intense light. I didn't care though—it still looked amazing."

★★★★☆

Activity type: Tour

SAILING THE SOLAR WIND

Hitch a ride across the solar system on a spaceship driven by the solar wind—the stream of particles flowing out of the Sun and across space at 90 miles (145 km) a second. Attach enormous, flimsy mirror-films to your craft for a relaxing sail through the wonders of space.

FLY THROUGH A
SUNSTORM

The surface of the Sun churns with rising heat and occasionally explodes outward with unimaginable power in a sunstorm. For the ultimate adventure sport, try sundiving. In a specially equipped ship, swoop low above the searing surface and duck through fiery columns and arches held up by magnetic fields. If you're lucky, your pilot might even fly you through a twisting loop of solar plasma.

Giant loops
Solar prominences can be more than 100 times bigger than planet Earth.

Cool plasma
The plasma in a prominence is cooler than the Sun's surface below it.

TOURIST TIP

Sun cycles

"Go at the right time.
The Sun goes through 11-year cycles of activity, so for the most impressive displays of sunspots and explosions make sure you book your trip during the high season."

Attraction type: Natural wonder

YOU ARE
HERE

SUN

MERCURY

VENUS

EARTH

MARS

ASTEROID BELT

JUPITER

Solar arch
These huge rings of plasma are called prominences.

Tricky task
You will need an experienced pilot for this dangerous adventure.

SOLAR POWER

The Sun generates enough energy every second to power human civilization for 500,000 years.

MAGNETIC STORM

As you swoop close to the Sun you'll notice some of your spaceship's instruments acting strangely. The Sun has an incredibly strong and changeable magnetic field. It twists and turns, creating the impressive sunspots and solar flares that can be seen across the surface.

 SATURN
 URANUS
 NEPTUNE
 PLUTO
 COMET
 NEBULA
 RED GIANT
 BLACK HOLE

9

NEED TO KNOW

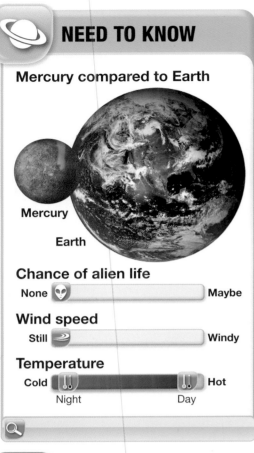

Mercury compared to Earth

Mercury

Earth

Chance of alien life

None ——————————— Maybe

Wind speed

Still ——————————— Windy

Temperature

Cold ——————————— Hot

Night   Day

THE SMALLEST PLANET

▶ Journey time from Earth: **5 months**

Mercury is the closest planet to the Sun. It whizzes around the star in only 88 Earth days, giving it the shortest year of any planet. If you enjoy sunbathing, Mercury is an ideal destination, with 2,000 hours of sunshine between sunrise and sunset. It takes 176 Earth days between sunrises, so one day on Mercury is twice as long as its year!

EXPLORE CALORIS BASIN

At 900 miles (1,500 km) in diameter, Caloris Basin is one of the largest craters in the solar system. When it formed, almost 4 billion years ago, it sent shockwaves across Mercury, creating strange rock formations on the opposite side of the planet.

Recent impacts ....
Lighter areas on Mercury indicate fresh craters, where the surface has been smashed to dust.

MERCURIAN MINISTRY OF TOURISM

MERCURY

OCTOBER 04, 2049

PLEASE TREAT OUR PLANET WITH RESPECT

Giant crater
The Caloris Basin is nearly one-third the width of Mercury itself.

Small is beautiful.

Visit the smallest planet in the solar system for the biggest sunsets!

Flat plains
Low-lying regions were flooded with lava, creating flat plains.

On Mercury you'll get **two years older** every day. That's an awful lot of **birthday parties.**

☁️ TEMPERATURE DROP

Mercury has a very thin atmosphere and, as a result, has the largest temperature swings of any planet. It can be 750°F (400°C) during the day but plunges to –290°F (–180°C) at night. It's worth packing a coat.

Cratered surface
The Mercurian landscape appears similar to the cratered highland areas of Earth's Moon.

SUNRISE ON MERCURY

If you're in the right place at the right time, you can see something amazing on Mercury: a double sunrise. Because Mercury's day is longer than its year, the Sun moves in strange ways across the sky. Seen from the right location, it rises in the morning, dips back below the horizon, and then pops back up again.

TOURIST TIPS

Comet spotting

"Awesome!
We watched a comet dive right into the Sun!"

Attraction type: Orbital tour

Double sunrise

"Be patient!
The double sunrise looked amazing, but the Sun's movement is agonizingly slow—allow at least a month to see it."

Attraction type: Solar display

Crater rim
For a great view across the landscape, climb the rim of any large crater—there are plenty to choose from.

Cool in the shade
The Sun's heat can be ferocious on Mercury, but the temperature in the shade is always well below zero.

SUN

YOU ARE HERE

MERCURY

VENUS

EARTH

MARS

ASTEROID BELT

JUPITER

Giant Sun
The Sun looks nearly three times larger from Mercury than from Earth—a truly spectacular sight.

Ghostly glow
There's almost no air on Mercury to block your view of the Sun's ghostly outer atmosphere—the corona. See its beautiful glow just before sunrise, after which the Sun's dazzling light will blot it out. You can also see the corona from Earth during an eclipse.

Scarface
Being near the Sun, Mercury has been pounded by asteroids and comets captured by the Sun's gravity, and its face is scarred by craters. The larger ones filled in with molten rock to form smooth "seas" like our Moon's.

Hot rocks
Mercury's rocky ground becomes scalding after sunrise. Insulated boots are a must.

VENUS

Venus compared to Earth

Venus   Earth

Chance of alien life

None 👽 ▣ ──────── Some

Gravity

Low ──────🔩──── High

Temperature

Cold ────────🌡️── Hot

🔍

A PLANET WITH ATMOSPHERE

▶ Journey time from Earth: **2–4 months**

The deadliest of the solar system's inner planets, Venus is like Earth's evil twin. It's about the same size as Earth and made of the same stuff, but it's hotter than a pizza oven on the surface and the air is so thick it can crush you to death in seconds. You'll need the best safety gear money can buy to visit Venus.

Below the clouds ·············
Dense clouds of acid cover Venus, but this false-color NASA image reveals what the geography below is like.

Land of volcanoes ····
The pink areas are highlands, which are packed with towering volcanoes. Eruptions are rare but enormous.

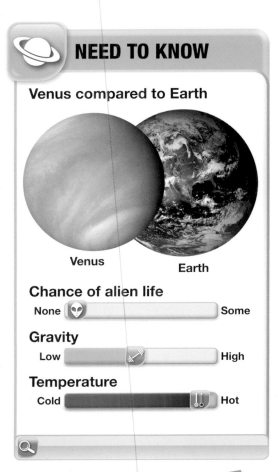

Take a balloon trip

Venus's fast-moving cloud layer will whizz you all around the planet in just four days!

Venus is the **hottest planet in the solar system**, with a surface temperature of **860°F** (460°C).

TOURIST TIP

Honeymoon getaway

"Honeymoon horror!
We booked our honeymoon here because Venus is named after the Roman goddess of love. But it couldn't be less like heaven!"

★★★★☆

Activity type: Surface landing

CLOUDY SKY

Venus is smothered by sickly colored clouds of sulfuric acid. There's never a break in the cloud, so it's permanently overcast below. At the bottom of the cloud layer, the temperature and pressure are about the same as on Earth, which makes this spot a great place to cruise in your ship or take a balloon ride for views of the surface.

Lava plains
Blue areas are flat, rocky plains formed from ancient lava floods.

If you **phone home** from Venus, your voice will take up to **15 minutes** to travel across space to Earth. Stick to **email** if you need to communicate!

Curly canyons
The highlands are riddled with winding valleys where volcanic activity has torn the ground open.

GETTING THERE

You can get to Venus in a few weeks when the planet is near to Earth in its orbit. Leave at the wrong time, however, and you'll waste a year flying around the Sun.

PANCAKES

Venus is a world of volcanoes. Its surface is covered with odd structures formed from solidified lava, such as the famous "pancake domes." These seven overlapping rock domes are each about 16 miles (25 km) wide.

VALID FOR ONE VENUSIAN DAY (243 EARTH DAYS)

VENUS
MARCH 22, 2025

THE VISITOR PERMISSION TO LAND ON VENUS

VENUS TOURIST BOARD—THIS STAMP GRANTS

LAND ON
MOUNT MAXWELL

If you've got the gear to cope with searing heat and crushing pressure, a great spot to land on Venus is Mount Maxwell, the planet's highest point. At 7 miles (11 km) high, its peak is taller than Mount Everest and provides fantastic views. The air is slightly cooler here, with a temperature of just 716°F (380°C)—although that's still hot enough to melt lead.

Under the weather
Don't worry about clouds blocking your view from the mountain—the cloud base on Venus is an amazing 28 miles (45 km) high.

LAVA LAND

Venus's top attractions are its volcanoes. They're everywhere, but no one is sure how many are active, since the thick clouds block our view from the Earth. Bring a camera—you might be lucky enough to snap some photos of glowing lava falls or explosive eruptions seen from your vantage point on Mount Maxwell.

Venusian air is so heavy that a gust of wind can **knock you** off your feet. Don't even think about taking a walk if the weather is **windy.**

16

SUN

MERCURY

YOU ARE HERE

VENUS

EARTH

MARS

ASTEROID BELT

JUPITER

Hazard warning
Keep away from volcanic
ash and dust. It may look
harmless, but it could contain
scalding vaporized lava.

Peak district
Mount Maxwell is not a
single mountain but a vast
mountain range stretching
for 530 miles (850 km).

TOURIST TIP

Heat haze

"Scorching!
It's like being in a giant oven, but
the weird views through the heat
haze make it worthwhile. Bring
plenty of chilled drinks to cool
down after your walk!"

★ ★ ★ ★ ★

Activity type: Mountain tour

VISIT VENERA

In 1983, a Russian space probe
called *Venera 13* parachuted through
Venus's dense clouds and touched
down on the roasting surface. It took
the first-ever color photo of Venus,
revealing a wasteland of broken rock
and dust. *Venera 13* was built like a
tank but survived only two hours in
the heat. If you want to visit what's
left of it, fly to the Phoebe Regio area.

SATURN

URANUS

NEPTUNE

PLUTO

COMET

NEBULA

RED GIANT

BLACK HOLE

17

NEED TO KNOW

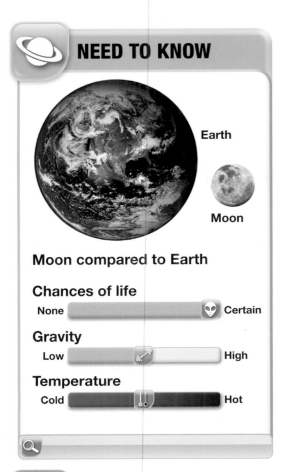

Earth

Moon

Moon compared to Earth

Chances of life

None ━━━━━━━━ Certain

Gravity

Low ━━━━━━━━ High

Temperature

Cold ━━━━━━━━ Hot

TOURIST TIP

Mid-Atlantic Ridge

"The floor was moving!
Earth is the only place in the solar system where the surface is made up of several moveable plates. We dived down to the bottom of a lake in Iceland to see new crust forming."

★★★★☆

Activity type: Scuba diving

THE LIVING PLANET

▶ Journey time from Earth: **0 hours**

It may seem boring to some space tourists, but there is no more vibrant planet to visit than our very own Earth. This green and blue world is the only planet in the solar system that's covered by huge oceans of water and teeming with complex forms of life.

Stormy weather
Cyclones such as this one in the Pacific Ocean tend to form in tropical regions of the planet.

Around **6,000** different **languages** are spoken on Earth—so bring a **phrase book.**

SUN

MERCURY

VENUS

YOU ARE HERE

EARTH

MARS

ASTEROID BELT

JUPITER

SOLAR ECLIPSE

Even though the Sun is much farther away from Earth than the Moon, they appear to be the same size in the sky from Earth because of the Sun's huge diameter. Once in a while, the Moon passes in front of the Sun, blocking out its light in an incredible solar eclipse.

Oceans
Water covers 71 percent of Earth's surface.

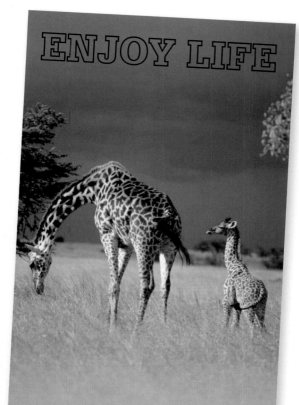

ENJOY LIFE

Earth is the only planet in the solar system where you're **GUARANTEED** to see living creatures!

EXPLORE METEOR CRATER

Travel to Meteor Crater in Arizona to see one of the most impressive impact craters on Earth. It was created 50,000 years ago by a rock from space. There are fewer craters on Earth than most other planets, since its surface is constantly changing because of erosion and geological activity.

SATURN

URANUS

NEPTUNE

PLUTO

COMET

NEBULA

RED GIANT

BLACK HOLE

MISSION TO
THE MOON

Our Moon is the largest moon in the solar system relative to its parent planet. There's a lot to see here, from gigantic meteorite craters to "seas" of flat rock formed from lava floods billions of years ago. Only four days away, the Moon is the perfect destination for a short break or for your first experience of an alien world.

Bay of Rainbows
This ancient crater filled up with lava billions of years ago, forming what now looks like a bay.

📷 DON'T MISS

Earthrise
The must-see sight after you arrive in lunar orbit is the view back to Earth. Watch our beautiful blue home world emerge like magic over the barren horizon. Not a sunrise, but an Earthrise!

Far side
The Moon always keeps the same face toward Earth, so we don't see its far side—but you can from orbit. The far side has few "seas" but lots of huge craters. Some experts think its craters were formed long ago by a second smaller moon that smashed into it.

Hills and hollows
Be sure to take a hike or buggy ride through the Moon's rolling hills, which are found around the rims of the big craters.

Rather than flying in a **straight line** to the Moon, you have to follow a figure-eight pattern, first **orbiting** Earth and then orbiting the Moon.

			YOU ARE HERE			
SUN	MERCURY	VENUS	EARTH	MARS	ASTEROID BELT	JUPITER

Apollo 15 landing site ✗

Apollo 17 landing site ✗

Apollo 11 landing site ✗

Sea of Tranquillity
The dark patches on the Moon, called "seas," are flat, dust-covered plains.

Craters
The Moon was battered by meteorites long ago, leaving thousands of craters. The largest is 1,300 miles (2,100 km) wide.

Lunar eclipse

"Stunning!
We arrived just in time for a lunar eclipse. The Sun disappeared behind the Earth, and Earth's atmosphere lit up like a neon light, changing from blue to orange to red."

Attraction type: Natural wonder

VISIT THE APOLLO LANDING SITES

Don't miss out on an unforgettable trip to one of NASA's famous Apollo landing sites. It was on these dusty plains that humankind first stepped onto another world. Try your shoe size against Neil Armstrong's footprint!

Apollo 15 lander
The Apollo 15 astronauts arrived on the Moon in this lander in 1971. Only the top half of the craft flew back into orbit. The bottom half, covered in gold foil, is still on the Moon today.

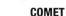

NEED TO KNOW

Mars compared to Earth

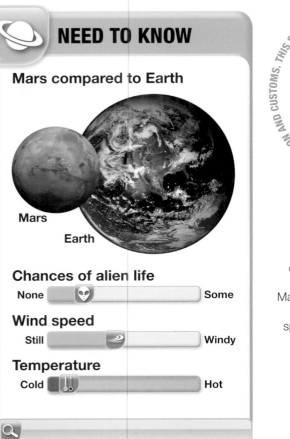

Mars

Earth

Chances of alien life

None ← [slider] → Some

Wind speed

Still ← [slider] → Windy

Temperature

Cold ← [slider] → Hot

DUST STORMS

When Mars is closest to the Sun, huge dust storms appear, sometimes covering the entire planet. Bring goggles so you can see clearly—and find your spaceship.

Volcano ·····
With huge central craters easily visible from space, the Martian volcanoes are among the most spectacular sights to see from orbit.

Sea of sand ·········
A great place to try sand skiing, this vast, sandy plain is dotted with large dunes.

MARS

THE RED PLANET

▶ Journey time from Earth: **7 months**

Mysterious Mars once had water and perhaps even life, but today this small desert world is frozen and dead. Seen from orbit, its face is scarred by huge volcanoes and a vast canyon complex. The dusty sky is pink rather than blue, and the air is too thin to carry sound far, creating an eerie silence.

22

 SUN

 MERCURY

 VENUS

 EARTH

YOU ARE HERE
 MARS

 ASTEROID BELT

 JUPITER

Lost river

In the distant past, water flowed north along this Martian river valley.

Once every two years there's a short **launch window** when Mars is **easiest to reach**. Make sure you're packed in time— you don't want to miss it!

TOURIST TIP

Canyon trip

"Fantastic!

Valles Marineris canyon is a must see. We used a buggy to explore the shallower slopes and then flew jetpacks into the deeper gullies! It is 2,500 miles (4,000 km) long though, so it took a while..."

Activity type: Canyon tour

Grand canyons

Called Valles Marineris, this huge canyon complex is Mars's answer to the Grand Canyon on Earth, but it's 10 times longer and four times deeper.

South pole

Like Earth, Mars has frosty poles where ice collects in winter. Unlike Earth's polar ice caps, those on Mars are made of carbon dioxide as well as water.

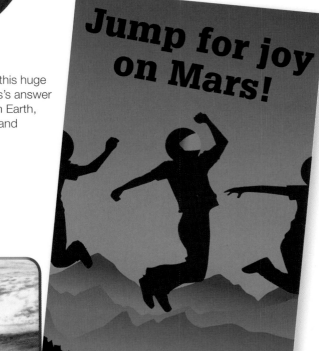

Jump for joy on Mars!

You can jump three times higher on Mars than on Earth due to its weak surface gravity.

MOUNTAIN CLIMBING

The extinct volcano Olympus Mons is three times taller than Mount Everest, making it the largest mountain in the solar system. It's so big, if you stand at the base you won't be able to see the summit because it will be over the horizon! Hike to the top or land there for stunning views into the crater.

 SATURN

URANUS

NEPTUNE

PLUTO

 COMET

 NEBULA

RED GIANT

 BLACK HOLE

Canyon trek

"Tired legs…
I bet my friend that I could walk
the whole length of the canyon.
I didn't realize it was 2,500 miles
(4,000 km) long!"

★★★★★

Activity type: Walking tour

HIKE ALONG THE
VALLES MARINERIS

One of the best hiking trips in the solar system
is along the edge of the Valles Marineris canyon.
Stretching nearly a quarter of the way around
Mars, it makes Earth's Grand Canyon look like
a tiny scratch in comparison. The channels
appear to have had water flowing down them
in ancient times, so look for fossils.

Landslides
Collapsing loose
ground and dust
storms continue to
shape this canyon.

MORNING MIST

If you get up early in the morning you might see mist collecting at the bottom of the valley. It's thought that water that froze on the ground the previous night is vaporized by the morning sun, creating a truly spectacular sight.

This giant canyon was named after the *Mariner 9* **space probe** that first photographed it.

Giant cliffs
Layers of sedimentary rock make up the walls of the valley.

Valley depth
Valles Marineris reaches up to 5 miles (8 km) deep in places.

CLIFF JUMP!
Parachute down from one of the highest cliffs. The air is very thin, so bring a supersized parachute to make sure you land in one piece.

TREK AROUND
VICTORIA CRATER

There are thousands of craters on Mars, some of them billions of years old. These scars made by falling space rocks last far longer here than on Earth because there's no rain to wear them away. A great one to visit is Victoria Crater, which is about the size of a football stadium.

Cape Victory

Mini crater
Look for this mini crater on the rim—it's only a few yards wide.

Sofi Crater

TOURIST TIP

Alien safari

"Boring!
We spent three days looking for alien life, but all we found were rocks. The tour guide said they might contain fossilized bacteria. Whatever!"

★★★★★

Attraction type: Safari

0   50 meters

0   100 feet

SUN

MERCURY

VENUS

EARTH

YOU ARE HERE
MARS

ASTEROID BELT

JUPITER

pe Pillar

Duck Bay

Spot the rover
Photographed from orbit in 2006, NASA's *Opportunity* rover is visible here as a dot.

Bottomless Bay

Bay of Toil

Cape Desire

Cape of Good Hope

Valley Without Peril

Cape St Vincent

Soup Dragon

Windswept rock
These dark streaks are areas of bare rock cleared of sand and dust by wind.

MARTIAN ROVER

In 2004, two robotic rovers from NASA landed on Mars to explore the surface. The baby-buggy-sized *Opportunity* rover spent two years trundling around Victoria Crater examining rocks and sending photos back to Earth.

CRATER FUN

Tire tracks
See if you can find *Opportunity*'s tracks and follow them around the crater. Fresh tracks and footprints on Mars are red. Martian dust is red because it contains iron oxide—rust!

Sandboarding
If you bring skis or a sandboard, you can have lots of fun riding down Martian dunes in low gravity. The dunes look just like those back home, but the sand is finer.

SATURN

URANUS

NEPTUNE

PLUTO

COMET

NEBULA

RED GIANT

BLACK HOLE

27

ASTEROID BELT

NEED TO KNOW

Asteroids compared to Earth's Moon

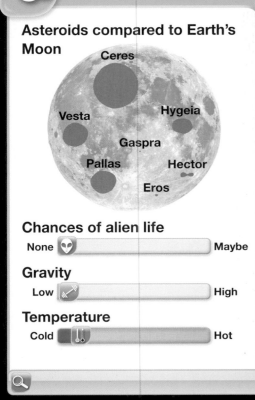

- Ceres
- Vesta
- Hygeia
- Gaspra
- Pallas
- Hector
- Eros

Chances of alien life

None ——————— Maybe

Gravity

Low ——————— High

Temperature

Cold ——————— Hot

A MILLION LITTLE WORLDS

▶ Journey time from Earth: **10 months**

As you travel between Mars and Jupiter you'll come across a region of space known as the asteroid belt. Here, millions of rocks orbit the Sun. Asteroids are usually too small for gravity to mold them into perfect balls like the planets. Instead, they are lumpy and shaped like potatoes.

Gaspra
This was the first asteroid to be studied in detail by a visiting spacecraft.

Toutatis
Asteroid Toutatis makes a close flyby of Earth every four years.

You'll need a tour guide!

The asteroid belt is mostly empty space. Without a guide, you won't see anything!

TOUR GUIDE

Some asteroids **rotate** in just a few hours. Standing on one of these **tiny worlds** could make you feel very **sick**, since the universe appears to **spin** over your head.

ASTEROID BELT TOURISM BOARD. THIS STAMP GRANTS FREE PASSAGE TO EVERY ASTEROID

ASTEROIDS
SEPTEMBER 1, 2083

EXCEPT CERES, WHERE AN ADDITIONAL FEE IS REQUIRED

28

 SUN

 MERCURY

 VENUS

 EARTH

 MARS

YOU ARE HERE
 ASTEROID BELT

 JUPITER

Make sure you **clip on a safety line** when **exploring** an asteroid, otherwise you could **jump** straight **off into space.**

TOURIST TIP

Bone world

"*How strange...* We were surprised to find that the asteroid Kleopatra is shaped like a dog bone."

⭐⭐⭐⭐⭐

Attraction type: Day trip

EXPLORE CERES

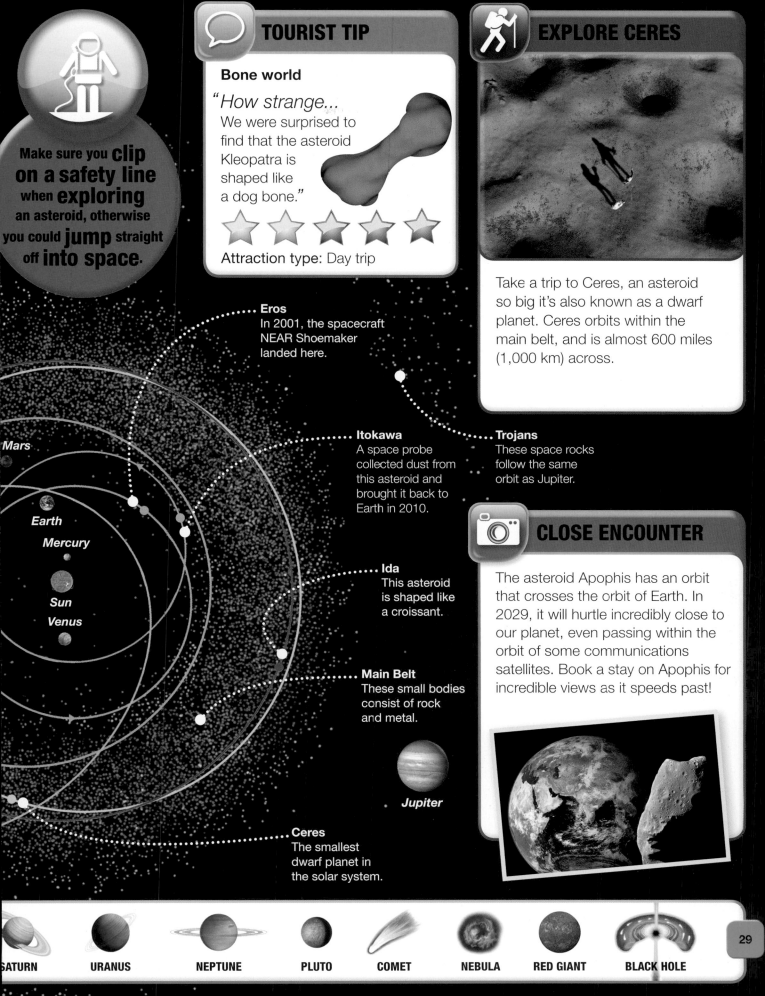

Take a trip to Ceres, an asteroid so big it's also known as a dwarf planet. Ceres orbits within the main belt, and is almost 600 miles (1,000 km) across.

Eros
In 2001, the spacecraft NEAR Shoemaker landed here.

Mars

Earth

Mercury

Sun

Venus

Itokawa
A space probe collected dust from this asteroid and brought it back to Earth in 2010.

Trojans
These space rocks follow the same orbit as Jupiter.

CLOSE ENCOUNTER

The asteroid Apophis has an orbit that crosses the orbit of Earth. In 2029, it will hurtle incredibly close to our planet, even passing within the orbit of some communications satellites. Book a stay on Apophis for incredible views as it speeds past!

Ida
This asteroid is shaped like a croissant.

Main Belt
These small bodies consist of rock and metal.

Jupiter

Ceres
The smallest dwarf planet in the solar system.

SATURN   URANUS   NEPTUNE   PLUTO   COMET   NEBULA   RED GIANT   BLACK HOLE

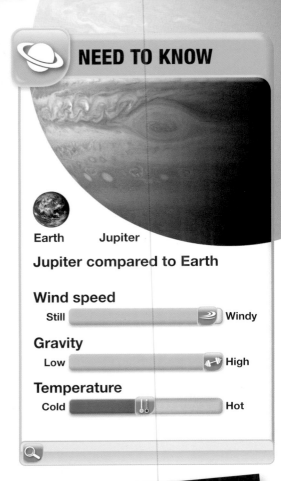

Earth   Jupiter

Jupiter compared to Earth

Wind speed

Still ———————————— Windy

Gravity

Low ———————————— High

Temperature

Cold ———————————— Hot

JUPITER

THE GIANT PLANET

▶ Journey time from Earth: **13 months**

Jupiter is the largest planet in the solar system and an essential stop-off on your trip. A gas giant, it's a world almost entirely made up of air. Violent storms whip around the planet at incredible speeds, which makes a trip to Jupiter fraught with danger. While you're here, make sure you visit Jupiter's incredible moons, Io and Europa.

TRIPLE ECLIPSE

The shadows cast by the moons of Jupiter as they pass over its clouds look fantastic. If you're really patient, you might catch three moons passing in front of the Sun at the same time in a triple eclipse. This happens once every four years.

You'll never get bored on Jupiter

With 63 moons, there's plenty to see!

Cloud colors
The different colors in Jupiter's clouds come from chemicals such as ammonia, hydrogen sulfide, and water.

Great Red Spot
This hurricane is three times larger than Earth and has been raging for more than 300 years.

YOU ARE HERE

Cloud bands
Bands of clouds race around the planet and storms are common where they meet.

North pole
Visit Jupiter's north pole to witness its beautiful auroras.

TOURIST TIP

Asteroid flight

"Scary...
If dodging asteroids is your thing, head over to the Trojan asteroids, which share the same orbit as Jupiter. Quite impressive, but I would skip it if you've already seen the asteroid belt."

★ ★ ★ ★ ☆

Attraction type: Tour

JOVIAN IMMIGRATION. ENJOY YOUR STAY

ON THE LARGEST PLANET IN THE SOLAR SYSTEM

JUPITER
MAY 14, 2029

ANY ISSUES, CONTACT OUR HELPDESK OFFICE ON EUROPA

AMAZING AURORA

Put on your ultraviolet goggles to see one of the most incredible sights in the solar system. Auroras occur on Jupiter's poles when charged particles from the volcanoes of Io collide with the planet's atmosphere.

Don't even think about flying close to Jupiter without a very powerful engine—you could get dragged in by the gigantic planet's gravity.

ATURN

URANUS

NEPTUNE

PLUTO

COMET

NEBULA

RED GIANT

BLACK HOLE

TOURIST TIPS

Colorful clouds

"Mesmerizing!
I could gaze for hours at the churning clouds of Jupiter—they're always changing."

★★★★☆

Activity type: Orbital tour

Thunder thrills

"Scary!
After the silence of outer space, the deafening thunder and roaring winds of Jupiter's storms was quite a thrill, but a bit frightening!!"

★★★★☆

Activity type: Storm cruise

Jupiter is surrounded by **lethal** radiation. Make sure your radiation **shields** are working or you'll be **DEAD** before you even reach the cloud tops.

Swirly colors
Watch out for the fantastic multicolored patterns that form between neighboring bands of cloud.

CLOUD CANYON

For the ultimate thrill, pilot your ship into the "cloud canyon" that surrounds the Great Red Spot. This deep chasm is free of cloud and offers a ringside view of the greatest storm in the known universe. Just remember to dodge the lightning bolts.

SUN

MERCURY

VENUS

EARTH

MARS

ASTEROID BELT

YOU ARE HERE

JUPITER

STORMCHASING ON JUPITER

Jupiter looks calm from a distance, but don't be fooled. Fly your ship into the clouds and you'll discover a world of incredible activity. Screaming winds tear through the sky at 250 mph (400 kph), whipping swirling gases and clouds into towering thunderstorms. Brace yourself for lightning bolts more powerful than any on Earth, torrential rain, and blizzards of chemical snow.

Great Red Spot
Don't count on this monster storm actually being red—it keeps changing color and sometimes fades to white.

In a spin
Watch the Great Red Spot for a while and you'll notice it spins around counterclockwise, dragged by winds moving opposite ways above and below it.

Great white spot
Watch out, too, for white spots—high storms that float on top of the other clouds. Sometimes, two white spots will crash, merge, and change color.

ATURN

URANUS

NEPTUNE

PLUTO

COMET

NEBULA

RED GIANT

BLACK HOLE

Io's largest volcanoes spray ash and sulfur **300 miles** (500 km) into space, creating **vast plumes** of falling debris. Bring an iron-clad umbrella!

TOUCHDOWN ON IO

Io is the most tortured moon in the solar system, its insides being constantly pushed and pulled by the immense force of gravity from nearby Jupiter. This makes Io violently volcanic. It has more than 400 active volcanoes, lakes of bubbling lava, and a surface covered by colorful splotches of sulfur and other chemicals belched out from within it.

34

 SUN

 MERCURY

 VENUS

 EARTH

 MARS

 ASTEROID BELT

 YOU ARE HERE

 JUPITER

Red hot
The temperature can reach 2,400°F (1,300°C) in Io's eruptions, so keep your distance!

Cosmic pizza
"Smothered in blobs of red, orange, and yellow, Io looked a bit like a pepperoni pizza!"

★★★★☆

Spot the difference
"Io's surface changes with every eruption. Don't buy a map—it will be out of date by the time you get here."

★★★★☆

Moon walk
It's safe to walk on much of Io. The surface is so cold that falling lava freezes quickly, forming solid ground.

LAVA LAKES

Take a tour of Io's sizzling lava lakes, including gigantic Lake Loki, which is 120 miles (200 km) wide.

"The Jupiter system's hottest attraction!"
Space News

Submarine tour

Take a submarine trip through Europa's hidden ocean and look out for any volcanic hot springs on the seafloor. Some scientists think these may be home to alien life.

Iceberg riding

From time to time, Europa's ocean melts through to the surface, creating a pool of open water that soon freezes over. If you're lucky enough to spot one of these water eruptions, hop a ride on one of the great drifting slabs of iceberg before they all freeze in place again.

Water world

"Utterly incredible!

We didn't find alien life, but the dark ocean under the huge roof of ice was an astonishing sight."

Attraction type: Scuba safari

Scuba gear

You'll need a fully airtight, pressurized diving suit for Europa. The water is exceptionally cold, so your suit will need built-in heating, too.

36

 SUN

 MERCURY

 VENUS

 EARTH

 MARS

ASTEROID BELT

YOU ARE HERE

 JUPITER

ICE DIVING ON EUROPA

Jupiter's moon Europa is encased in solid ice and has the smoothest surface of all the solar system's worlds. But beneath this frozen shell is a hidden ocean with more liquid water than all of Earth's oceans and lakes combined. Bring diving gear—this is the best place in the solar system to search for alien life.

Don't worry about **falling** through **thin ice** if you land on Europa's surface. In most places, the icy crust is miles thick!

Roof of ice
Don't miss the view of the roof of ice over your head. You'll need a flashlight to see though it—there's no sunlight in Europa's deep dark sea.

GIANT CRACKS

Take a close look at Europa's surface from orbit. You'll see very few craters, but lots of strange, crisscrossing lines that run all around the globe. These are deep cracks in the ground. They are caused by Jupiter's powerful gravity kneading Europa's insides.

 SATURN
 URANUS
 NEPTUNE
 PLUTO
 COMET
 NEBULA
 RED GIANT
 BLACK HOLE

37

SATURN

Saturn compared to Earth

Earth

Saturn

Chance of life
None ⬤ ─────────── Some

Wind speed
Still ──────── ⬤ ── Windy

Temperature
Cold ⬤ ───────── Hot

LORD OF THE RINGS

▶ Journey time from Earth: **2 Earth years**

The second-largest planet in the solar system, Saturn is a gas giant like Jupiter. It's most famous for its beautiful rings, but it also has a system of more than 60 varied and interesting moons, many of which are worth a trip. If you visit the Saturn system, don't miss the moons Titan and Enceladus.

Earth

💬 TOURIST TIP

Saturn flyby

"*Wow!*
The most majestic planet of all, Saturn is the greatest sight in the solar system. The rings are dazzling when they catch the sunlight, yet look paper thin when you fly in line with them. The main planet is fascinating, too, with swirling storms and stripes of cloud like Jupiter's."

★ ★ ★ ★ ☆

Attraction type: Saturn system tour

Saturn's shadow
Fly past Saturn's dark side for a stunning view of the rings lit from behind by the Sun.

 SUN

 MERCURY

 VENUS

 EARTH

 MARS

 ASTEROID BELT

 JUPITER

DON'T MISS

Ringside view

To see Saturn's rings in all their glory, fly through the planet's cloud tops near the equator. You'll see the vast rings arching high overhead, with streaks of cloud shooting under them.

Sponge world

Saturn's large family of moons includes a few oddballs. Hyperion was the first non-round moon that astronomers discovered. It has so many deep, sharp-edged craters that it looks like a giant bath sponge.

Bulging waistline
Saturn spins so fast, taking only 10 hours to rotate, that its middle bulges outward.

Despite being **gigantic**, Saturn has very low **density** and would actually **float** in water—if you could find a bucket **big** enough.

LIGHTNING

Be sure to check the weather before you venture into Saturn's cloudy skies. It has the longest lightning storms in the solar system. They last for months and produce lightning 10,000 times more intense than those on Earth.

TOURIST TIP

Cassini Division

"Watch out!
This looks like a huge black gap in the rings, but it actually contains lots of small boulders. I wish someone had warned me!"

⭐ ⭐ ⭐ ⭐ ⭐

Attraction type: Orbital tour

JET SET!

Fly a jet pack through the gaps in Saturn's rings to see the rings from both sides.

"A unique way to view this incredible wonder"

Ringmaster
Saturn is 4,350 miles (7,000 km) below its closest rings.

Pockmarks
The ice particles are covered in pockmarks from collisions with each other.

40

SUN

MERCURY

 VENUS

 EARTH

MARS

 ASTEROID BELT

 JUPITER

SURF THE RINGS OF SATURN

One of the best reasons to visit Saturn is to see its phenomenal rings. Made up of millions of chunks of ice, they sparkle in the light of the Sun, creating one of the most beautiful sights in the solar system. Don't miss a spectacular ride through this natural wonder.

Ice boulder
You can land on the largest blocks of ice, which are as big as a house.

YOU ARE HERE

SATURN

URANUS

NEPTUNE

PLUTO

COMET

NEBULA

RED GIANT

BLACK HOLE

41

TOUCHDOWN ON
TITAN

Saturn's moon Titan is giant-sized, even larger than the planet Mercury. It is the only moon to have a thick atmosphere and the sky is filled with dense orange smog. The perfect destination for sailing vacations, Titan is the only place in the universe other than Earth that we know has lakes and oceans on its surface. They aren't filled with water though, but with liquid chemicals such as methane and ethane.

Take to the skies

The thick air and low gravity on Titan means you can strap wings to your arms and fly away!

Titan's surface
Titan is so cold that water is frozen as hard as stone and makes up much of the moon's landscape.

SUN

MERCURY

VENUS

EARTH

MARS

ASTEROID BELT

JUPITER

WEIRD RAIN

The rainstorms are huge here so pack a good umbrella. It's strange though—because of Titan's low gravity and thick atmosphere, the rain droplets grow to the size of marbles and then drift gently down to the ground.

Orange smog
Titan is a dark and gloomy world because smog blocks out most of the sunlight.

Methane lakes
These lakes are perfect for a relaxing boat trip.

The liquid in the lakes is **much lighter** than water. If you fell **overboard** you'd **sink** pretty quickly, especially wearing a **heavy spacesuit.**

YOU ARE HERE

SATURN

URANUS

NEPTUNE

PLUTO

COMET

NEBULA

RED GIANT

BLACK HOLE

43

One of Saturn's rings is formed of ice from the fountains of Enceladus.

📷 GLITTER BALL

Don't miss the stunning views of Enceladus glittering in the sunlight when you're in orbit around this moon. Also look for the dark "tiger stripes" where the icy crust has split.

Ice canyon
The fountains erupt from deep valleys called tiger stripes, which give Enceladus a striped appearance when seen from space.

💬 TOURIST TIP

Fountain tour

"Awe-inspiring!
A mind-blowing sight. The ice gushes out of the ground at an amazing speed, and with no air and little gravity to slow it down, it seems to keep on rising forever."

⭐⭐⭐⭐⭐

Attraction type: Natural wonder

Gravity is so weak on Enceladus, you'll weigh less than a pineapple does on Earth. Make sure you **harness** yourself to the ground so you don't go flying off!

SUN   MERCURY   VENUS   EARTH   MARS   ASTEROID BELT   JUPITER

THE FOUNTAINS OF ENCELADUS

If you want to visit some of Saturn's 62 moons, Enceladus should be top of your list. This tiny, ice-coated moon is the shiniest, whitest world in the solar system. Astronomers used to think it was just a boring snowball, but in 2005 they discovered huge eruptions of glittering ice from valleys in its surface—the fountains of Enceladus.

Eruption site
The fountains are fed by an underground salty sea near the moon's south pole.

AROUND THE MOON IN ONE DAY

Take a snowmobile trip and drive all around tiny Enceladus in just 24 hours. Watch the cracks though!

YOU ARE HERE

 SATURN

 URANUS

 NEPTUNE

 PLUTO

 COMET

 NEBULA

RED GIANT

 BLACK HOLE

45

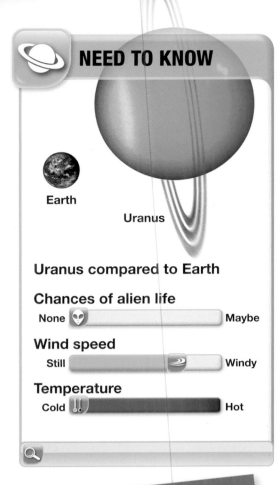

Earth

Uranus

Uranus compared to Earth

Chances of alien life

None — Maybe

Wind speed

Still — Windy

Temperature

Cold — Hot

URANUS

THE SIDEWAYS PLANET

▶ Journey time from Earth: **4 Earth years**

Uranus is possibly the most boring planet in the solar system. You can't visit its surface and there aren't any storms—just a plain covering of blue-green clouds of methane. There is something unusual about Uranus, though: it's the only planet in the solar system to roll along on its side rather than spinning around upright. If you're stuck for things to do, head to Uranus's moon Miranda, where you can climb the tallest cliffs in the solar system.

Cloud cover · · · · · · · · ·
The white bands in Uranus's atmosphere are the highest clouds.

Chill out on Uranus

It's the coldest planet in the solar system. Temperatures get as low as –371°F (–224°C).

WACKY SEASONS

Because Uranus rolls around on its side, it has some extremely unusual seasons. Each pole gets 42 years of continuous daylight followed by 42 years of night. Keep this in mind when planning your trip—it's much more interesting on the sunny side.

 SUN

 MERCURY

 VENUS

 EARTH

 MARS

 ASTEROID BELT

 JUPITER

Brightest ring
Epsilon is the outermost of Uranus's inner rings, and also the brightest.

URANUS
JANUARY 19, 2066

A RELAXING VACATION DESTINATION. NO TERRIFYING STORMS OR SCARY VOLCANOES HERE. — WELCOME TO URANUS.

Uranus is **1.8 billion miles** (3 billion km) from the **Sun** and takes **84** years to **orbit** it.

Blue planet
Methane crystals in the atmosphere absorb red light, making Uranus blue.

TOURIST TIP

Boring planet

"What a waste of time!
Scientists think that soon after Uranus formed, an Earth-sized planet smashed into it, knocking it on its side. Unfortunately, nothing that exciting happens here anymore. There's nothing to do!"

★ ★ ★ ★ ☆

Attraction type: Tour

BULLSEYE

It's not only Uranus that has been tipped over, but its rings and all of its moons, too. Look out of your ship window as you approach the planet and you'll see the faint rings tilted toward you like a giant bullseye.

CLIMB THE CLIFFS OF MIRANDA

The best of Uranus's icy moons is Miranda, which has the tallest cliffs anywhere in the solar system. Pack your ice ax and crampons and try scaling the 5-mile (8-km) tall cliff face—the views over the moon and beyond are breathtaking. To get back down, simply jump off the top and fall all the way. In the weak gravity, it will take seven minutes to get to the base, but you'll need a jetpack to break your fall.

The inner moons of Uranus are in **unstable orbits** and may **collide** with each other one day, so **watch out!**

Twilight world
The Sun is so far from Miranda that daylight feels more like twilight. Bring a flashlight to find the way.

For a romantic getaway ...

... why not try Uranus's miniature moon, Cupid, named after a Roman god of love!

 SUN   **MERCURY**   **VENUS** EARTH **MARS**   **ASTEROID BELT**   **JUPITER**

Uranus's rings ......
The view of Uranus and its
faint rings is spectacular
from Miranda's surface.

TOURIST TIPS

Uranus has 27 known moons. Here
are reviews of some of the largest.

Ariel

"The brightest of Uranus's
mostly dark moons, Ariel
has deep canyons filled
with glittering ice."

★★★★☆

Titania

"Titania is named after a fairy
queen in a Shakespeare play.
It's the ideal place from which
to send artsy postcards!"

★★★★★

Oberon

"Weird—if you look at the
Sun from Oberon, the Sun
goes around and around in
the sky in small circles."

★★★★☆

**YOU ARE
HERE**

ATURN   URANUS   NEPTUNE   PLUTO   COMET   NEBULA   RED GIANT   BLACK HOLE

NEPTUNE

Neptune compared to Earth

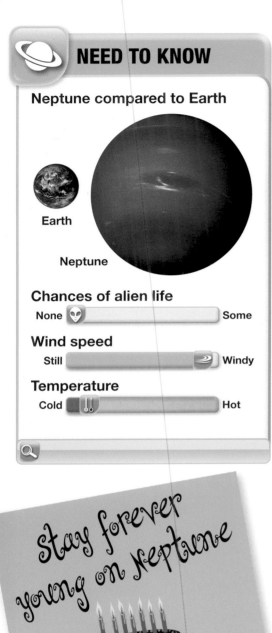

Earth

Neptune

Chances of alien life

None ─────────────── Some

Wind speed

Still ─────────────── Windy

Temperature

Cold ─────────────── Hot

THE WINDY WORLD

▶ Journey time from Earth: **8 Earth years**

Neptune is the farthest planet from the Sun and it is not for the fainthearted. Freezing, perilous storms rage throughout Neptune, unlike its relatively calm neighbor Uranus, making it a dangerous place to visit. While here, make sure you stop off at the nearby moon Triton to visit its fantastic geysers.

Blue planet
Neptune appears blue because the methane in the upper atmosphere absorbs the red light from the Sun, but reflects the blue light.

Stay forever young on Neptune

One year on Neptune lasts **165 Earth years**, so you'll always stay your current age!

SUN

MERCURY

VENUS

EARTH

MARS

ASTEROID BELT

JUPITER

DIAMOND RAIN

Far beneath your spaceship in Neptune's gas interior, there are showers of gemstones falling like rain. The extreme heat and pressure can transform the methane gas into diamonds.

NEPTUNE TOURIST BOARD—THIS STAMP GRANTS

VALID FOR ONE NEPTUNE YEAR—IF YOU LAST THAT LONG!

THE VISITOR A FREE STAY ON NEPTUNE OR TRITON

NEPTUNE
MARCH 22, 2025

SOAR THROUGH THE ATMOSPHERE

Take to the skies with a hang glider and catch the powerful winds in Neptune's atmosphere. They are the strongest in the solar system, reaching 1,250 mph (2,000 kph), so brace yourself for a hair-raising ride.

Storms
Storms rage throughout Neptune's atmosphere.

Cloud bands
A bit like Jupiter, Neptune has bright and dark cloud bands running around the planet.

YOU ARE HERE

ATURN   URANUS   NEPTUNE   PLUTO   COMET   NEBULA   RED GIANT   BLACK HOLE

HAVE A BLAST ON
TRITON

Do you want to get your feet back onto solid ground? Visit Triton, Neptune's largest moon. Its volcanic geysers are one of the natural wonders of the solar system. Stand back and watch as nitrogen gas erupts up to 5 miles (8 km) above Triton's scarred face. Don't worry if you arrive on Triton later than expected—each eruption can last for up to a whole Earth year, so you'll have plenty of time to soak up the view.

Erupting gas
The nitrogen gas that erupts from the geyser is quickly blown away by the wind.

Geyser debris
The geysers leave dark streaks on Triton's surface that stretch for hundreds of miles.

SUN

MERCURY

VENUS

EARTH

MARS

ASTEROID BELT

JUPITER

Neptune has 12 other moons you can also visit. Here are the best of the bunch.

Proteus

"We visited a really cool crater that was more than 125 miles (200 km) in diameter."

Neso

"Terrible trip. We had to travel 30 million miles (48 million km) from Neptune just to get here. It took ages…"

Naiad

"We couldn't stay long because it's going to smash into Neptune's atmosphere soon!"

Orbiting Neptune

Triton is the only large moon in the solar system that orbits in a different direction from its planet's rotation.

SATURN

URANUS

YOU ARE HERE

NEPTUNE

PLUTO

COMET

NEBULA

RED GIANT

BLACK HOLE

53

PLUTO

Pluto compared to Earth

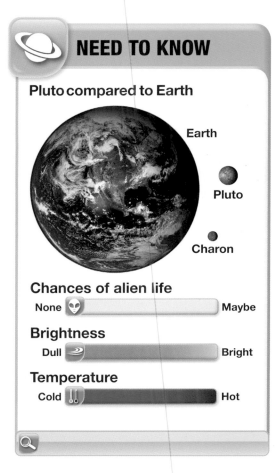

Earth

Pluto

Charon

Chances of alien life
None 👽 ▬▬▬▬▬ Maybe

Brightness
Dull ▬▬▬▬▬ Bright

Temperature
Cold 🌡️ ▬▬▬▬▬ Hot

THE DWARF PLANET

▶ Journey time from Earth: **9-10 Earth years**

Pluto is a small and frosty world lurking in the outer solar system. You'll notice that Pluto's moon Charon is extremely large in comparison to Pluto—they're like double worlds twirling around each other. In 2006, astronomers decided that Pluto wasn't an actual planet, but a dwarf planet, along with Eris and Ceres. However, it's still well worth a visit.

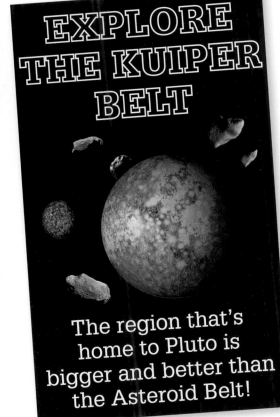

Patchy surface ......
Different parts of Pluto are covered in water ice, frozen nitrogen, and frozen methane.

STARLIGHT

When you finally reach Pluto, the Sun will look like no more than a bright star in the sky, and as a result, it's dark on Pluto's surface. It's easy to get lost on Pluto—bring a flashlight to help you explore.

EXPLORE THE KUIPER BELT

The region that's home to Pluto is bigger and better than the Asteroid Belt!

SUN

MERCURY

VENUS

EARTH

MARS

ASTEROID BELT

JUPITER

Orange world
Although Pluto is a frozen world, it's a dirty orange color.

If you're planning to go ice-skating, make sure you **cool** your skates down first. The frozen nitrogen could **explode** beneath your feet with just a little **warmth**.

HEAD FOR A SLED

Head over to Charon to go sledding. Unlike Pluto, its surface consists mostly of ice, which makes for a safer ride. The gravity is far lower on Charon than on Pluto though, so be careful not to sled off into space.

TOURIST TIP

Short stay on Pluto

"Cold and dark…
I don't know why I bothered—Pluto isn't even a planet anymore! I'd recommend visiting the dwarf planet Eris instead—it's bigger."

⭐⭐⭐☆☆

Attraction type: Tour

ENTITLES YOU TO A FOUR-MONTH STAY ON PLUTO · THE BEST DWARF PLANET IN THE SOLAR SYSTEM

PLUTO
OCTOBER 22, 2103

YOU MIGHT AS WELL VISIT CHARON WHILE YOU'RE HERE

SATURN

URANUS
NEPTUNE
YOU ARE HERE

PLUTO

COMET
NEBULA
RED GIANT
BLACK HOLE

55

TWIN TAILS

Most comets have two tails pointing in slightly different directions. The brightest tail is made of dust and curves back along the comet's orbital path. The second tail, which is often blue, is made of gas and always points directly away from the Sun, whichever way the comet is flying.

Choose your comet **carefully**—some comets don't just **swoop** around the **Sun,** they **crash** into it!

RIDE A
COMET

Comets are big lumps of dirty ice that normally lurk unseen in the outer solar system but occasionally come swooping close to the Sun. As a comet nears the Sun, it warms up and comes to life. Ice and dust erupt from its surface to form a huge, glowing cloud around the comet and spectacular tails. If you've got plenty of time on your hands, you can hitch a ride on a comet in the outer solar system and travel all the way around the Sun.

SUN

MERCURY

VENUS

EARTH

MARS

ASTEROID BELT

JUPITER

LAND ON A COMET

Make sure you land on the solid core, or nucleus, of the comet. It's best to do this while the comet is in the outer solar system, beyond Jupiter. Once it gets as close to the Sun as Mars, its fragile surface will begin to break up, releasing fountains of gas and dust that will cloud your view. The icy surface of the comet is actually pretty dark because the ice contains lots of other chemicals, including amino acids—the building blocks of life.

Tall tails
The tails of comets can grow millions of miles long as comets near the Sun, but disappear when comets fly back to the outer solar system.

Watch your feet when **strolling** on a comet—**sudden eruptions** of gas can happen without warning and **blast** you into space!

TOURIST TIP

Comet landing

"*Dirty snowball*
A comet is like a giant snowball, so we thought it would be the ultimate place for a snowball fight. But there was so much gunk around that the snow was black."

★ ★ ★ ★ ☆

Activity type: Comet cruise

Blue and violet regions
This is where gas reflects the light from hot, young stars.

Green light
Radiation from young stars makes oxygen produce green light.

SWING BY A
STARBIRTH NEBULA

▶ Journey time from Earth: **20 million Earth years**

Seen from Earth, a nebula is just a blurry smudge, but as you approach one you'll see it is actually a vast colorful cloud of gas and dust. The Orion Nebula is situated in the Orion constellation. Thousands of new stars and the planets that orbit them are forming in regions of the cloud.

SUN

MERCURY

VENUS

EARTH

MARS

ASTEROID BELT

JUPITER

NEW PLANETS

Many young stars have dusty disks swirling around them, where new planets are forming. Visit one to witness the birth of a new world. Some of these planets may one day evolve life of their own.

Red regions.....
Radiation from new stars makes hydrogen glow red.

TOURIST TIP

Pillars of Creation

" Absolutely incredible!

We visited the Eagle Nebula in the Serpens constellation to see the Pillars of Creation. Stars were forming within the gigantic columns of gas, and we could see some poking out of the top."

☆ ☆ ☆ ☆ ☆

Activity type: Sightseeing

The **Orion Nebula** is **1,300 light-years** away from **Earth**. A light-year is how far **light can travel** in one year.

SATURN

URANUS

NEPTUNE

PLUTO

COMET

YOU ARE HERE

NEBULA

RED GIANT

BLACK HOLE

59

TRAVEL TIP

Red giant tour

"Spooky!
The starlight makes everything look blood red—it's really spooky! It was a very long trip, but we spent most of it asleep in deep freeze."

★★★★☆

Attraction type: Interstellar cruise

Betelguese is one of the **largest red giants** known. If you swapped it with the **Sun**, its surface would reach all the way to Jupiter!

Scorched planet
The heat of a red giant or supergiant turns nearby planets into scalding, waterless desert worlds. One day, this will happen to Earth.

SUPERNOVA

When Betelgeuse reaches the very end of its life, it will self-destruct in an explosion brighter than a billion suns—a supernova. Its core will then collapse under gravity until it's only a few miles wide. Betelgeuse could explode any time in the next million years. When it does, it will outshine the Moon in Earth's night sky.

 SUN

 MERCURY

 VENUS

EARTH

 MARS

 ASTEROID BELT

 JUPITER

VISIT A DYING STAR

▶ Journey time from Earth: **10 million Earth years**

Once a star runs out of fuel, it begins to die. Its outer layers puff outward enormously and cool to a red color. The star becomes a "red giant" or a "red supergiant"—a bloated, dying star hundreds of times bigger than our Sun. Betelgeuse (pronounced "beetle juice") is one of the nearest red supergiants and definitely worth a visit.

Supersize star
As a dying giant star swells up, it swallows the planets and moons around it.

GETTING THERE

Betelgeuse is in the constellation of Orion, and you can see its reddish color easily from Earth. The star is 640 light-years from Earth, which means that its light takes 640 years to cross space to reach your eyes. Your ship can't travel anywhere near as fast as light speed. At the speed of NASA's fastest-ever space probe, it would take you 10 million years to fly to Betelgeuse.

Betelgeuse

SATURN

URANUS

NEPTUNE

PLUTO

COMET

NEBULA

YOU ARE HERE
RED GIANT

BLACK HOLE

JOURNEY TO A BLACK HOLE

▶ Journey time from Earth: **94 million Earth years**

When a gigantic star dies, all its matter gets sucked by gravity into a single point that's tinier than the period at the end of this sentence. The star turns into a black hole, a dark monster with such powerful gravity that not even light can escape its clutches. Only the most daring space tourist should consider flying near a black hole.

Point of no return
Anything crossing this line is trapped inside the black hole forever—even light. Astronomers call the line the "event horizon."

🚀 LONG-HAUL FLIGHT

The nearest black hole is 6,000 light-years away from Earth. Traveling at the speed of NASA's *Voyager* spacecraft, it will take you 94 million years to get there. Your body will have to be frozen during this long voyage, so you don't age.

Doomed stars
Some black holes tear apart and suck in the stars around them, growing ever more powerful as they swallow more matter.

📷 GALACTIC CENTER

At the center of our galaxy is a black hole so massive that it weighs more than a billion Suns. The black hole itself is invisible, but it's surrounded by a violent whirlpool of debris from torn up stars.

SUN

MERCURY

VENUS

EARTH

MARS

ASTEROID BELT

JUPITER

Keep your distance

"Scary!
Well before we reached the event horizon, we felt the awesome pull of the black hole's gravity and had to turn back. Don't get too close or it could tear your ship apart."

Attraction type: Interstellar cruise

If you fell into a black hole, you'd be **stretched** into a long, thin strand—a gruesome process known as spaghettification.

Center point
All the matter in a black hole is concentrated into one point in the center, called a "singularity." It is so small, it has zero size.

INDEX

ACKNOWLEDGMENTS

Dorling Kindersley would like to thank Richard Beatty for proofreading and Chris Bernstein for the index.

The publisher would also like to thank the following for kind permission to reproduce their photographs:
(Key: a-above; b-below/bottom; c-centre; f-far; l-left; r-right; t-top)
Alamy Images: CVI Textures 16clb. **Corbis**: Mike Agliolo 10clb; Jonathan Blair 19crb; Yvette Cardozo / Index Stock 36-37; Dennis di Cicco 56clb; Miloslav Druckmuller, Vojtech Rusin / Science Faction 13cra; Larry Dale Gordon 10crb; Mehau Kulyk / Science Photo Library 60clb; Mark Garlick Words & Pictures Ltd / Science Photo Library 40cla; Weatherstock 39crb; Jim Zuckerman 19tr. **Dorling Kindersley**: 50tl;

50-51. **Dreamstime.com**: Diego Barucco 53ftr. **ESA**: NASA / G. Bacon (STScI) 62-63; NASA, and M. Showalter (SETI Institute) 46tl, 47l. **ESO**: L. Calçada / http://creativecommons.org / licenses / by / 3.0 54clb. **Getty Images**: Flickr / Celisa B. M. Serra 21tr; The Image Bank / Werner Van Steen 35cr; Eric Meola 51crb (hang glider); Stocktrek Images 25tc. **NASA and The Hubble Heritage Team (AURA / STScI)**: ESA, and E. Karkoschka (University of Arizona) 30c; ESA, John Clarke (University of Michigan) 31br. **Japan Aerospace Exploration Agency (JAXA)**: 7crb. **Ron Miller**: 12-13, 15ftr, 16-17, 22bl, 24-25, 29tr, 32clb, 34-35, 39ca, 40-41, 44-45, 48-49, 51tr, 51crb, 52-53, 55cra, 57crb, 60cl, 60-61, 62crb. **NASA**:

9crb, 17crb, 21br, 24cl, 53tr; Cassini Imaging Team / SSI / JPL / ESA 38-39; Cassini-Huygens / JPL / Space Science Institute 39cra; ESA / Paolo Nespoli / Dmitry Kondratyev 4-5 (background); ESA / SOHO 6-7; Goddard Space Flight Center Image by Reto Stöckli (land surface, shallow water, clouds). Enhancements by Robert Simmon (ocean color, compositing, 3D globes, animation). Data and technical support: MODIS Land Group; MODIS Science Data Support Team; MODIS Atmosphere Group; MODIS Ocean Group Additional data: USGS EROS Data Center (topography); USGS Terrestrial Remote Sensing Flagstaff Field Center (Antarctica); Defense Meteorological Satellite Program (city lights) 10tl, 14tl, 18tl, 22tl (Earth), 30tl

(earth), 38tl (Earth), 46fcla, 50ftl, 54tl; GSFC / NOAA / USGS 18-19; Dr. Joe Gurman / US SOHO Project Scientist / NASA Goddard Space Flight Center 6tl; Jeff Hester and Paul Scowen Arizona State University 59br; Jet Propulsion Laboratory (NASA-JPL) 27tr; Jet Propulsion Laboratory / California Institute of Technology, Pasadena, CA / David Seal 46crb; Johns Hopkins University Applied Physics Laboratory / Carnegie Institution of Washington 11c, 13cr; Johnson 20cl; JPL 15br, 15fbr, 30clb, 32-33, 37br; JPL / DLR 30cl; JPL / Mosaic by Mattias Malmer 14ftl, 15tr; JPL / NSSDC Photo Gallery 36ca; JPL / Space Science Institute 30tl, 30-31, 38ftl, 44cl; JPL / University of Arizona 27br, 35tc, 35tr, 36clb, 53tl; JPL / USGS 14-15, 20-21t; JPL-Caltech / Cornell University 27cr; JPL-Caltech / T. Pyle (SSC) 59cra; JPL-Caltech / University of Arizona / Cornell / Ohio State University 26-27;

Lunar and Planetary Institute 20-21b; Mariner 10; Astrogeology Team, U.S. Geological Survey 10ftl; NSSDC / GSFC 20bl; Stephen Ostro et al. (JPL), Arecibo Radio Telescope, NSF 29tc; SDO / AIA 8-9; Viking Project 22tl (Mars), 22-23; Voyager 2 47crb. **naturepl.com**: Wild Wonders of Europe / Lundgre 18bl. **Science Photo Library**: Chris Butler 56-57; Russell Croman 58-59; David Ducros 15cr; Walter Myers 11crb; John Sanford 61crb. **Luc Viatour (www.lucnix.be) (CC BY-SA 3.0)**: http://creativecommons.org/licenses/by/3.0 19ca.

End papers: Corbis: Robert Llewellyn.

All other images © Dorling Kindersley
For further information see:
www.dkimages.com